STEPHEN JAMES

Social Media for Schools

A practical guide to using social media to improve parental engagement

The power of social media lies in its ability to connect and engage with people in a meaningful way. By harnessing the potential of social media, schools can build strong relationships with their community, promote their values and ethos, and support student learning and achievement.

Stephen James BA(Hons), QTS, FRSA

Contents

Acknowledgement

I want to express my heartfelt gratitude to Seabrook Church of England Primary School (Folkestone), St. Martin's Church of England Primary School (Folkestone), Phoenix Community Primary School (Ashford), Trinity Catholic High School (Woodford Green) and Hartsdown Academy (Margate) for being my first clients and true trailblazers. Their encouragement and belief in me have been instrumental in helping me to establish my business and to further understand the importance of social media in education.

I would also like to thank Ronel Lehmann, CEO of Finito Education, for his invaluable coaching, mentoring, and constant encouragement. His guidance and support have been valuable in helping me to grow my business and ultimately complete this book.

I am also profoundly grateful to my friends and family for their support and encouragement throughout the writing process. Their love and encouragement have been a constant source of inspiration and strength.

Introduction

Social media has become a ubiquitous presence in our daily lives, with over 3 billion people worldwide using various platforms to connect, share information, and stay up-to-date on current events. In the UK alone, it is estimated that around 68% of the population uses social media, with the highest usage among young people aged 16-24 (Office for National Statistics, 2021).

As educators, we understand the constant pressure to communicate effectively with our communities and provide learning opportunities beyond the classroom. Parental engagement is critical in this regard, as it has been shown to have a positive impact on student achievement and overall school success (Education Endowment Foundation, 2021).

Social media can offer a convenient and engaging way to improve parental involvement, promote our values and ethos and reinforce classroom learning.

But how can we effectively harness the potential of social media in education? This book aims to explore the benefits of social media from an educator's perspective and provide practical tips for integrating it into your school or institution. By the end, you'll have a better understanding of what your school may have been missing out on and how social media can transform your teaching and learning practices, particularly regarding increasing parental engagement.

Let's get started.

1

Getting Started

In Chapter One, we will delve into the importance of effectively using social media to tell your school's story. With so many schools competing for attention, it is crucial to stand out and create a unique, engaging presence that showcases what makes your school special. Social media offers a quick and convenient way to provide an authentic window into the daily life of your school, allowing outsiders to gain an insight into what your school has to offer and why it stands out from the rest.

Regular updates and posts from real people can build a genuine relationship between your school and the community, improving communication with parents and strengthening your school's identity and culture. Studies have shown that increased parental engagement can positively impact student achievement (Hoover-Dempsey et al., 1995; Farrell, 2010), and using social media to share student successes and involve parents in everyday school life can improve the overall reputation and sense of community within your school. It can also create a sense of pride and esprit de corps among students, teachers, and parents.

However, it's essential also to be aware of the potential risks associated with social media and to have appropriate policies in place to ensure the safety of students and staff. It is crucial to have a specialist in online safety, such as our CEO Stephen James, a trained CEOP Ambassador, to help navigate the complexities of social media and ensure that you can fully utilise its benefits for your school while minimising any negative impacts.

Why schools use social media.

1. ***Improving parental engagement****: Schools can use social media to communicate with parents and keep them informed about their child's education. Using social media, schools can encourage parents to get involved in their child's education and stay informed about school events and activities. There are several reasons why a school might use social media, including:*
2. ***Communication****: Social media can be a quick and effective way for schools to communicate with students, parents, and staff. Schools can use social media platforms like Facebook, Twitter, and Instagram to share important updates, announcements, and information.*
3. ***Marketing****: Schools can use social media to promote their events and other activities to a broader audience. Schools can use social media to reach out to potential students and families and showcase their offerings.*
4. ***Professional development****: Some schools may use social media as a professional development tool for teachers. For example, teachers can use social media to connect with other educators and share resources and best practices.*

Private and state schools often have different goals and priorities compared to state schools. Private schools may focus more on marketing to attract students, generate income, and promote charitable endeavours, while state schools may prioritise parental engagement. However, private and state schools can use social media to achieve various goals, including communication, marketing, and professional development.

The Benefits

There are several benefits for schools that use social media, particularly regarding parental engagement and pupil outcomes (Education Endowment Foundation, n.d.). Social media can be a quick and effective way for schools to communicate with parents, providing them with updates, announcements, and important information about their child's education. This can help to improve parental engagement and involvement in their child's learning. By using social media, schools can also provide parents with access to resources and information to support their child's education at home. In addition, social media can facilitate collaboration between parents, teachers, and students, allowing them to communicate and share ideas more easily. This can lead to increased engagement and improved learning outcomes for students.

According to a report by the Education Endowment Foundation (EEF, 2022), parental engagement can positively impact pupil outcomes. The report found that interventions that aim to increase parental engagement in their child's learning can lead to an average of four additional months' progress for students.

Change perceptions

Social media can be a valuable tool for changing perceptions about a school, particularly in the case of a poor inspection grade or a school scandal. In these situations, the school needs to take control of its brand narrative and use social media to communicate its message effectively.

One way to do this is through 'psychological operations', which involve using persuasive techniques to influence the attitudes and behaviour of target audiences. This can include creating a positive and engaging online presence, using clear language, and messaging, and highlighting the strengths and achievements of the school. It is also essential for the school to be transparent and open in its communication and to address any concerns or issues head-on. This can help build trust and credibility with stakeholders and show that the school is committed to positive changes.

Using social media to change perceptions about a school requires careful planning and strategy. By taking control of its brand narrative, using persuasive techniques, and being transparent and open in its communication, a school can use social media to change negative perceptions and rebuild trust with stakeholders effectively.

School's Social Media Manager

Managing your school's social media presence can be challenging and risky, but it is important in today's digital world. There are a few options to consider when it comes to this task. One option is to outsource the work to a social media marketing agency specialising in working with schools and improving parental engagement. In this case, choosing an agency run by qualified teachers, such as Social Media for Schools, is beneficial to ensure that the content and messages are appropriate and align with your school's values and goals.

Another option is to handle your school's social media in-house. In this case, it is crucial to designate a highly skilled and capable staff member, preferably a qualified teacher, as your Social Media Manager (SMM). The SMM should have advanced technical skills to manage the platforms, exceptional communication skills to engage with your audience and community, and the ability to monitor what is happening online constantly. They should also be aware of the best times to post and how to reach the widest audience while keeping all students safe.

The SMM needs to provide thorough training for all staff members on the role of social media in the school and how it should be used. This includes setting strict school policies on identifying students, reminding teachers not to tag pictures with real student names or post controversial content, and teaching teachers how to use the required technology to provide content.

A school social media manager manages the school's social media accounts and develops strategies to engage with students, parents, and other stakeholders. This role involves creating and scheduling content, responding to comments and messages, and analysing the performance of social media campaigns. This job description may help you:

Key responsibilities:

- *Develop and implement a social media strategy for the school, including goals, target audiences, and content themes*
- *Manage the school's social media accounts, including creating and scheduling posts, responding to comments and messages, and moderating discussions*
- *Analyse the performance of social media campaigns using tools such as Google Analytics and social media analytics platforms*
- *Collaborate with other members of the school community, including teachers, students, and parents, to create and share engaging content*
- *Stay updated with current trends and best practices in social media marketing.*
- *Support the school's overall marketing and communication efforts through social media*

Qualifications:

- *Experience as a school leader*
- *Experience in social media management, including creating and scheduling content, analysing metrics, and developing strategies*
- *Excellent communication skills, both written and verbal*
- *Strong organisational and time management skills*
- *Proficiency with social media platforms, including Facebook, Twitter, Instagram, and LinkedIn*

· *Familiarity with social media analytics tools and software*

Social Media Platforms.

Keeping your social media presence active and engaging is essential now that you have set up your social media platforms and trained your staff. To do this, it can be helpful to have a small team of teachers working alongside the designated Social Media Manager (SMM) to ensure that there is always someone available to post updates and respond to questions and comments from the community.

School Brand

Branding is an essential aspect of any business or organisation, and it is no different for schools. Creating a solid brand image and consistently delivering high-quality content can establish credibility and build recognition among your target audience. Social media is a powerful tool for enhancing brand identity and building relationships with your audience, and it is essential to use appropriate channels to engage with your followers consistently.

According to research, strong branding can lead to increased 'customer' loyalty and positive associations with a company or organisation (Jones, K. 2021). In the education sector, a strong brand can help attract new students and parents and foster a sense of community and pride among current students, staff, and alumni (McCausland, 2020).

To effectively leverage the power of social media for branding purposes, it is crucial to be consistent in your messaging and visuals and to communicate your vision and values as a school. This can involve using specific colours, fonts, and images in your posts and consistently posting high-quality content that aligns with your brand. By doing this, you can attract new students and build a robust social network of followers who recognise and appreciate your school's brand.

However, it is essential to remember that branding is not just about creating a positive perception of your school but also about consistently delivering excellent results and building credibility. Therefore, it is essential to carefully consider the content and messaging you share on social media and ensure that it aligns with your school's values and goals.

The Effects of Covid-19

The Covid-19 pandemic has significantly impacted how schools operate, and social media has played a crucial role in helping schools adapt to the challenges of remote learning and virtual communication. From live streaming events and filming important information videos to sharing updates and resources with students and parents, social media has provided a powerful platform for schools to stay connected and engaged with their community. This highlights the importance of having a strong social media presence and effectively using these platforms to connect with your community in times of crisis.

Conclusion

In this chapter, we have explored the importance of effectively using social media to tell a school's story and its various benefits. Here are the five key takeaways from this chapter:

- *Social media provides a quick and convenient way for schools to showcase their unique qualities and engage with their community.*
- *Regular updates and posts from real people can build a genuine relationship between a school and its community, improving communication with parents*

and strengthening the school's identity and culture.
- *Parental engagement can positively impact student achievement, and using social media to share student successes and involve parents in everyday school life can improve the overall reputation and sense of community within a school.*
- *Schools must be aware of the potential risks associated with social media and have appropriate policies in place to ensure the safety of students and staff.*
- *By understanding social media's benefits and potential risks, schools can effectively use this tool to engage with their community and achieve their goals.*

Social media is a powerful tool for schools looking to improve communication, parental engagement, and student outcomes. By using social media effectively, schools can create a robust online presence and connect with their community meaningfully.

2

The Benefits of Social Media for Your School

Social media has become an integral part of people's lives and can bring numerous benefits to schools. This chapter will explore how social media can help schools improve community engagement, promote their values and ethos, and provide a window into the classroom for families. We will also discuss how social media can be beneficial for teaching and help students learn and stay connected with their peers and school community. Finally, we will guide the next steps schools can take to use social media and maximise its benefits effectively.

With over 3.6 billion users on social media worldwide, schools could connect with and market themselves to a vast audience for free. While it may not be possible to reach that many people, social media can effectively reach your immediate school community and the broader geographical area. It can also attract new students, parents, and staff and establish your school as a community leader. By effectively utilising social media, schools can significantly enhance their reputation and impact on their local community.

Promoting Your School

Pupil Recruitment

To effectively use social media to recruit pupils, it is important to regularly post high-quality content that showcases the unique aspects of your school and what sets it apart from others. This can include images and videos of extracurricular activities, classroom learning, and school events. You can also use social media to share news and updates about your school, such as academic achievements or special initiatives, which can help to demonstrate a strong sense of community and pride at your school.

Additionally, it is crucial to be responsive to questions and comments from potential parents on social media. By promptly answering questions and engaging with your audience, you can create a positive perception of your school and build trust with potential parents.

Research supports the effectiveness of using social media for pupil recruitment. A study by the University of Kent found that schools that used social media as part of their recruitment strategy saw an increase in the number of applications and a higher quality of applicants (Wong, 2022). Another study found that social media can be an effective way for schools to target specific groups, such as disadvantaged or minority students, and increase diversity in the student body (Johnson, 2020).

Staff Recruitment

Using social media to advertise job openings can effectively reach a wider audience and attract qualified candidates to your school. Several platforms can be beneficial for promoting teaching positions, including:

- **LinkedIn:** *This professional networking site is a popular platform for job*

postings and is particularly useful for attracting experienced educators.
- ***Twitter****: By using relevant hashtags, such as #teachervacancy or #educationjobs, you can reach a larger audience of potential candidates.*
- ***Facebook****: This platform can be a valuable tool for reaching a larger audience, particularly if you have a strong presence on the platform and can use targeted advertising to reach specific groups of potential candidates.*

In addition to promoting job openings, showcasing the positive aspects of working at your school, such as the supportive team culture, professional development opportunities, and student achievements, is vital. This can help attract candidates who align with your school's values and are more likely to thrive in your school community.

Community Leadership

Schools are an integral part of any community and often serve as the first point of contact for many of the issues facing society. As such, schools need to take on a leadership role within their communities and use their social media platforms to signpost families and other community members to local resources, such as extracurricular activities, clubs, and events.

In addition to promoting local resources, schools can use their social media presence to raise awareness about critical social issues, such as mental health, well-being, and charity work. By effectively communicating and engaging with their community through social media, schools can strengthen their identity and build trust within the community.

According to a study published for the Pew Research Center (Duggan et al., 2015), schools that effectively use social media to engage with their community show higher levels of parent and community involvement, which can lead to improved student outcomes and overall school success. Therefore, headteachers need to consider the role of social media in promoting their school as a community leader and resource for families and community members.

Social Media in the Classroom

According to a study published in the Journal of Research in Science Teaching, social media can be an effective tool for professional development for teachers (Bruguera et al., 2019). In their research, Bruguera et al. (2019) found that teachers who participated in social media communities for educational purposes reported increased confidence in their teaching practices and a greater sense of connectedness to their colleagues.

Furthermore, social media can be an effective way to engage parents and build relationships with the school community; it can be an excellent way for teachers to connect with parents, share information and celebrate children's learning more immediately than traditional methods. By using social media to share updates, photos, and other information with parents, teachers can help build trust and improve communication with the school community.

The use of social media in the classroom can be a valuable tool for professional development and engagement with the school community. However, schools need clear policies and guidelines to ensure teachers' and students' safe and appropriate use of social media.

Outreach and Enrichment

Social media provides a massive opportunity for schools to reach out on behalf of students to a wide range of organisations that can enrich their student's learning. Authors, religious organisations, professional organisations, academics, politicians... all these groups can add value to subjects that children are learning, providing a deeper dimension to the learning process.

For example, you could use social media to:

- *Connect with an author while reading one of their books. Encourage your students to tweet or message the author with questions or comments about the book.*
- *Engage with local politicians or councillors while learning about British values. Encourage your students to ask questions or express their views on the topic.*
- *Promote women in engineering by finding and messaging female professionals in the field.*

Using social media, you can inspire your students to think beyond the classroom and connect with various individuals and organisations to enhance their learning experience. It's crucial to ensure that you have a team to manage these efforts effectively and follow best practices for online safety and communication.

Online Safety

Schools must lead by example and demonstrate best practices in online safety to their students and their communities. This can involve regularly educating students about online safety, creating and enforcing school policies on social media use, and promoting responsible online behaviour. According to a study published in the *British Journal of Educational Psychology*, teachers who model responsible social media use and promote it to their students can help create a safe and positive online community for students (Hayes B et al., 2022).

Using social media as a tool for education and positive reinforcement, schools can help students develop a healthy and safe relationship with technology. In addition to role modelling, schools can also utilise social media to educate students about online safety. This can include sharing resources and tips for staying safe online, promoting online safety events and campaigns, and sharing success stories of students who have demonstrated responsible social media use.

Conclusion

In conclusion, social media can be a powerful tool for schools looking to improve communication, promote their values and ethos, and provide a window into the classroom for families. By using social media effectively, schools can significantly enhance their reputation and impact on their local community. Social media can also benefit teaching and learning, allowing students to stay connected with their peers and school community and providing teachers with access to a wealth of resources and professional development opportunities.

Here are the five key takeaways from this chapter:

1. *Social media can be an effective way for schools to improve community engagement and reach a wider audience.*
2. *Schools can use social media to attract new students, parents, and staff by regularly posting high-quality content and engaging with their audience.*
3. *Social media can benefit teaching and learning, providing students with access to resources and teachers with professional development opportunities.*
4. *Schools must have appropriate policies to ensure students' and staff's safety and privacy when using social media.*
5. *Schools should develop a clear strategy to use social media effectively, establish a dedicated team or individual to manage their accounts, and regularly review and update their social media presence.*

Social media can be a valuable tool for schools looking to connect with their community, promote their values and ethos, and support teaching and learning. By understanding social media's benefits and potential risks, schools can use this tool to enhance their reputation and impact on their local community.

3

How to Run your School's social media

Social media can be a powerful tool for schools to connect with and engage their community, promote their school, and enrich the learning experience for students. However, it is crucial for school leaders to carefully consider their social media strategy and ensure that it is aligned with their school's values and goals. In this chapter, we will explore the benefits of social media for schools, best practices for managing social media accounts, and practical tips for engaging and supporting your school community. We will also discuss the importance of online safety, and the role schools can play in educating students and parents about responsible social media use. By following these best practices, school leaders can effectively leverage the power of social media to benefit their schools and positively impact their communities.

Your School's Strategic Aims

When running your school's social media accounts, you must consider what you want to achieve through these platforms. These strategic aims can often fall into several interlinking categories, including:

- ***Showcasing learning***: *social media is a great way to showcase the learning* *and achievements of your students. This can include sharing photos and videos of class projects, school trips, and other educational activities. By showcasing the learning at your school, you can demonstrate the quality of education your students receive and encourage others to consider enrolling their children at your school.*

- **Highlighting important curriculum areas**: *You can use social media to highlight specific areas to draw attention to. For example, you could share posts about a science fair or a history project your students are working on. This can be a great way to showcase the variety of educational opportunities available at your school.*

- **Promoting school values or religious values**: *If your school has specific values or a spiritual focus, social media is a great way to promote these to your community. You can share posts about events or activities that align with these values or include them in your regular content.*

- **Promoting PTA events and fundraising**: *Many schools use social media to promote events and fundraising activities organised by their Parent–Teacher Association (PTA). This can include sharing information about bake sales, carnivals, and other events and promoting online fundraising campaigns.*

- **A bridge between the formalities of school letters and newsletters**: *social media provides a more informal and interactive way to communicate with parents and the wider school community. It can be a great way to share updates and information that might not make it into more formal communication channels like school letters or newsletters.*

- **Showing the 'lighter side' of school life**: *In addition to sharing information about learning and school events, it can be helpful also to share posts that show the more fun and light-hearted side of school life. This could include sharing photos and videos of students participating in extracurricular activities, such as music or sports, or simply sharing posts that show the personality and culture of your school.*

- **Recruitment**: *social media is a valuable tool for attracting new students to your school. By sharing information about your school and the educational opportunities available, you can help to attract new families to your community.*

- **School community engagement**: *Social media can be a great way to foster a* *sense of community within your school. By encouraging parents and students to interact with your content and share their experiences, you can create a sense of belonging and connection within your school community.*

Your School Community

Researching your school community is essential in determining the best social media strategy for your school. Several ways to gather this information include speaking to parents at the school gate, asking the PTA for feedback, or conducting a formal survey through your normal school communication channels.

It is worth noting that different social media platforms tend to attract different demographics. According to UK-based statistics, Facebook is popular among parents, governors, and other school community members. However, Instagram is gaining popularity among younger parents. Twitter and LinkedIn are more commonly used by professionals in the education sector and can help share best practices and connect with other schools and educational organisations.

If you are starting with social media, Facebook and Twitter are good options for reaching a broad audience within your school community. As you gain more experience and want to expand your reach, you may want to consider using additional platforms such as Instagram and LinkedIn.

Remember that your school community is not limited to parents and students. It would be best if you also considered the local and global community in your school. By sharing information about your school and engaging with other educators and professionals on social media, you can position your school as a hub of best practices and establish valuable connections with others in the education sector.

Your School's Social Media Accounts

The first step in managing your school's social media presence is to conduct a social media audit. This involves reviewing any existing social media accounts set up for your school, including any that may be dormant or unofficial. It is essential to identify all these accounts to ensure that you have a comprehensive and accurate picture of your school's social media presence. Once you have completed the audit, you can begin setting up new social media accounts or reviving dormant ones.

- *Twitter is relatively straightforward, requiring only an email address and phone number (usually that of your designated Social Media Manager). You can customise the platform with your school's logo and start tweeting, following, and retweeting.*
- *Setting up a Facebook page is slightly more complex, as it requires the creation of a page (rather than a group). You can also add settings that allow you to moderate comments, add profanity filters, and various contact details. It is common for this page to be linked to a personal Facebook account, which can make some staff members uneasy. However, linking the page to a personal account is vital to access all the features and settings necessary for managing your school's social media presence effectively.*
- *Instagram is also a popular social media platform, particularly among younger users. You can customise your profile with your school's logo and start sharing photos and videos of your school and its activities. To set up an Instagram account, you must provide an email address, phone number, and username.*
- *LinkedIn is a professional networking platform that can be useful for connecting with other educators and professionals in the education sector. To set up a LinkedIn account, you must provide your name, email address, and password. You can customise your profile with your school's information and build your network.*

In our experience, Facebook and Twitter are the most popular social media platforms among schools in the United Kingdom.

In addition to reviewing and setting up social media accounts, it is also essential to consider the academic research and news articles relevant to your school's social media strategy. By staying up to date with the latest research and trends in social media and education, you can ensure that your school uses these platforms effectively.

Your School's Social Media Manager

Effective management of your school's social media presence requires a highly skilled and dedicated individual with diverse skills, including technical expertise, excellent communication skills for crafting written content, and a strategic vision for promoting your school's brand.

Branding is a complex and vital aspect of your school's social media strategy. It involves creating a unique identity that includes everything from your logo and colours to your mission and values. This process helps to differentiate your school from others and creates a cohesive and consistent image easily recognisable by your community.

Managing your school's social media accounts is a time-intensive task requiring great attention to detail. In addition to creating engaging and exciting content, your social media manager must monitor comments and replies to posts, responding promptly and professionally to any inquiries or concerns. This requires excellent communication skills and the ability to multitask effectively.

Many schools designate an office team member as the social media manager, but this person must have the time and resources to manage the account effectively. The role of social media manager is often too complex and demanding for a teacher to take on in addition to their other responsibilities.

Rushed or poorly thought-out content can damage your school's brand and reputation.

Your School's Posting Frequency

When managing your school's social media accounts, it is essential to strike a balance between posting frequently enough to engage your audience but not so often that you risk overwhelming them or diluting the impact of your messages.

Here are some general guidelines for how often you should post on different platforms:

- ***Facebook, Instagram, and LinkedIn****: One to two posts per day. These platforms are more conducive to longer-form content and visual media, so you can afford to post less frequently while maintaining a solid presence.*
- ***Twitter****: Four to five posts or retweets per day. Twitter is a more fast-paced platform, so you may consider posting more frequently to keep your school's presence in mind for your followers.*

To help manage your posting schedule and ensure that your content is spread evenly over a week or month, you may consider using a scheduling tool such as Hootsuite. This can save you time and help you plan for future posts.

Best Practices for Posting Frequency:

- ***Consider the attention span of your audience****: Your school community is likely composed of people with different levels of engagement with social media. Some may be avid users constantly checking their feeds, while others may only visit your accounts occasionally. When deciding how often to post, consider the attention span of your audience and aim to strike a balance between* *maintaining their interest and not overwhelming them with content.*

- ***Vary your posting frequency based on the platform****: Different social media platforms have different cultures and expectations regarding posting frequency. For example, Twitter is known for its fast-paced nature, while Instagram tends to focus on high-quality visual content. Consider these differences when deciding how often to post on each platform.*

- ***Use analytics to inform your posting frequency****: Many social media platforms offer tools that help you understand how your posts perform and how often you should post. By reviewing these analytics, you can better understand what works best for your school's audience and adjust your posting frequency accordingly.*

Your School's Positive and Engaging Narrative

Your school's social media profiles are a powerful tool for shaping the narrative about your school and showcasing what makes it unique. By carefully curating the content you share on these platforms, you can control the message you want to convey to your school community and beyond.

It is important to remember that social media is, well, social! Your accounts should not just be a stuffy rehashing of your school newsletter or a platform for announcing mundane updates. Instead, use your social media profiles to share fun and engaging content that captures the spirit and personality of your school.

Here are some examples of ways that you can create a positive and engaging social media narrative for your school:

- ***Share photos and videos of your students in action****: Showcase the creativity, enthusiasm, and accomplishments of your students by sharing photos and videos of them engaged in learning, extracurricular activities, and other* *activities that highlight their talents and interests.*

- ***Share stories about your staff and community****: Highlight the dedication and expertise of your team by sharing profiles, interviews, or other stories about their work and contributions to your school. You can also feature stories about your school's partnerships, collaborations, and community involvement to showcase your school's role in the local and global community.*
- ***Share news and updates about your school****: While you don't want your social media accounts to be a vehicle for mundane updates, it is still essential to keep your community informed about important news and developments at your school. Consider using a mix of formats, such as text, photos, and videos, to share updates about events, achievements, and other newsworthy items.*
- ***Have fun****: Don't be afraid to inject some fun and personality into your social media accounts. Consider using humorous or light–hearted content, such as memes, jokes, or quizzes, to engage your audience and show the lighter side of your school.*

Following these principles, you can create a positive, engaging social media narrative that reflects your school's unique culture and values.

Your school's response to Negative Comments

If you receive negative comments or complaints on your school's social media page, handling them professionally and effectively is essential. For more detailed guidance on handling these situations, please refer to Chapter 9, which covers this topic in more depth.

In general, here are some fundamental principles to keep in mind when dealing with negative comments on social media:

- *Stay calm and professional*
- *Acknowledge the statement and show that you are listening.*

- *Respond promptly to prevent the situation from escalating.*
- *Offer a solution or suggest a way for the person to get in touch with the appropriate person or department to resolve the issue.*
- *Use private channels if the comment is particularly sensitive or personal.*

By following these best practices, you can effectively manage negative comments on social media and maintain a positive and professional online presence for your school.

Monitoring

Effective management of your school's social media accounts requires regular monitoring and engagement. This includes responding to comments and inquiries and actively seeking out and amplifying positive mentions of your school.

On platforms like Twitter, building your following requires actively following others and participating in conversations. While this may seem simple, it can be time-consuming and requires a commitment to staying up to date with the latest trends and developments on the platform.

In addition to the time required to monitor your social media accounts, it is also essential to have a member of your school's leadership team responsible for overseeing the management of these accounts. This person should ensure that the shared content aligns with your school's strategic aims and is appropriate for your school community.

Failing to monitor your school's social media accounts properly can have serious consequences. If you do not promptly respond to comments or inquiries, you risk damaging your school's reputation and alienating your community. In addition, if you do not actively seek out and amplify positive mentions of your school, you may miss out on opportunities to promote your school and engage with your community.

Overall, monitoring your school's social media presence is a time-intensive task that requires careful planning and organisation. By setting clear goals and establishing clear roles and responsibilities, you can ensure that your school's social media accounts are managed effectively and efficiently.

Safeguarding

Ensuring the safety and well-being of children and staff is of the utmost importance when using social media in a school setting. As stated by the National Society for the Prevention of Cruelty to Children (NSPCC), "Digital technology provides children with a wealth of opportunities for learning and communication, but it can also expose them to risks such as bullying, grooming and access to inappropriate material" (NSPCC, 2021). This means that it is vital for schools to have clear policies in place for permissions to appear on social media, as well as safeguarding measures to protect against online risks.

One of the critical aspects of safeguarding on social media is managing personal information, including using student names and photos. The NSPCC recommends that schools use appropriate privacy settings and strict guidelines on using personal information, particularly for children (NSPCC, 2021). It is also essential to have a designated staff member, such as the head teacher or a senior leadership team member, responsible for monitoring your school's social media accounts and ensuring that they are being managed according to the school's policies and strategic aims.

To further support your school's efforts in safeguarding social media, it is essential to have a robust social media policy that outlines the expectations and guidelines for the responsible use of these platforms. This may include guidance on appropriate language and behaviour and procedures for handling any concerns or incidents that may arise.

As school leaders, embracing new technologies and leveraging their potential to strengthen your school's unique narrative and community is essential. A well-managed and active social media account can be a powerful tool for celebrating your school's achievements and creating a sense of community. By following best practices and adhering to safeguarding policies, you can use social media to improve your school's brand and increase parental engagement.

Conclusion

In conclusion, chapter three explored the critical considerations for managing a school's social media presence. By setting strategic aims, engaging with the school community, and maintaining a positive and engaging narrative, schools can effectively use social media to connect with their audience and promote their school. It is also essential to have a designated social media manager, establish a posting frequency, and have the plan to respond to negative comments. Safeguarding and monitoring are crucial aspects of social media management. Schools should have policies and procedures in place to ensure the safety of their students and the integrity of their online presence.

Key takeaways from this chapter include:

- *The importance of aligning a school's social media strategy with its strategic aims.*
- *The school community's role in shaping the content and tone of a school's social media presence.*
- *The need for a designated social media manager and a plan for responding to negative comments.*

By following the guidelines outlined in this chapter, schools can effectively manage their social media presence and create a positive and engaging online presence for their community.

4

Types of Posts to Share

From highlighting student achievements to promoting school events and resources, there are many ways that schools can use social media to create a positive online presence. This chapter aims to provide guidance on the types of content schools can share on their social media platforms to engage and inform their community. In this chapter, we will explore the different types of posts that schools can share and provide tips for crafting effective and engaging content. Whether you are a social media manager or a teacher looking to promote your school on social media, this chapter will provide valuable insights and ideas for creating a successful online presence.

Content Pillars

Content pillars are essential for several reasons. Regarding social media, content pillars help establish a clear focus for a school's content. Schools can create a consistent and cohesive message on social media by identifying a few key areas or themes that align with the school's mission and values. This can help to attract and engage followers who are interested in those specific areas, and it can also help to establish the school as a thought leader in those areas.

Content pillars can also help to streamline the content creation process. Schools can more easily plan and create content that aligns with those pillars by identifying a few key focus areas. This can save time and resources and help ensure that the shared content is relevant and valuable to the school's community.

Content pillars are essential for establishing a clear focus and direction for a school's social media presence and creating a consistent and cohesive message that resonates with followers and aligns with the school's mission and values. Here are 15 content pillars that schools might use:

1. *Student achievements and accomplishments*
2. *School community highlights*
3. *Classroom updates and highlights*
4. *Resources for students and families*
5. *Staff updates and highlights*
6. *Educational tips and resources*
7. *Behind-the-scenes looks at school life*
8. *School news and updates*
9. *Inspirational quotes and messages*
10. *Local Community opportunities*
11. *Extracurricular activities and clubs*
12. *School events and activities*
13. *Student wellness and mental health resources*
14. *Sustainability and environmental initiatives*
15. *PTA Fundraising*

Trusted Organisations

Social media can be a powerful tool for sharing information and engaging with communities, but it can also be a source of misinformation or false information. It is vital for schools to only share content from trusted organisations on social media to ensure the accuracy and reliability of the information being shared. By only sharing content from trusted organisations, schools can help ensure that the information they share is accurate and reliable.

Sharing content from trusted organisations can also help to build trust and credibility with the school's community. By demonstrating a commitment to sharing accurate and reliable information, schools can establish themselves as trusted source of information for their communities. Here are some examples of trusted organisations that we use at Social Media for Schools:

1. *Department for Education (DfE)*
2. *Child Exploitation and Online Protection Centre (CEOP)*
3. *YoungMinds*
4. *Local authorities*
5. *BBC*

Religious Content

Schools should acknowledge religious holidays on social media to show respect and inclusion for their community's diversity of beliefs and traditions. Celebrating religious holidays on social media can help to promote a culture of respect and acceptance within the school and can also serve as an opportunity for education and learning about different faiths and traditions.

By celebrating religious holidays on social media, schools can also show their support for the spiritual and cultural traditions of their students, families, and staff. This can help to build a sense of community and inclusivity within the school and can foster a positive and welcoming environment for all members of the school community. Here are some examples of a tweet that might be sent from a school:

1. *"Happy Easter to all of our students, families, and staff! We hope you have a wonderful day filled with love, joy, and time with loved ones."*
2. *"Wishing everyone a happy and blessed Eid al–Fitr! We are grateful to be a part of such a diverse and inclusive community."*
3. *"Wishing our students, families, and staff a happy Hanukkah! We hope you have a wonderful holiday filled with light, joy, and celebration."*
4. *"Happy Diwali to all of our students, families, and staff! May this festival of lights bring you joy, happiness, and prosperity."*
5. *"Happy Christmas to all of our students, families, and staff! We are grateful for all of our blessings and the opportunity to be a part of such a wonderful community."*

National Importance

Celebrating national holidays on social media to show pride and respect for the country's history, traditions, and values. Celebrating national holidays on social media can help to promote a sense of community and belonging within the school and can also serve as an opportunity for education and learning about the country's history and culture.

By celebrating national holidays on social media, schools can also show their support for the values and traditions of their country and can foster a positive and inclusive environment for all members of the school community. Here are some examples of a tweet that might be sent from a school:

1. *"Happy St. George's Day to all our students, families, and staff! We are proud to be a part of such a great country with a rich history and culture."*
2. *"On VE Day, our students and staff honour the sacrifices of those who fought for our freedom and democracy."*
3. *"Happy Burns Night to all our students, families, and staff! We celebrate Scotland's national poet's life, work, and enduring legacy."*
4. *"Happy St. Patrick's Day to all our students, families, and staff! We are grateful to be a part of such a vibrant culture."*
5. *"Happy Birthday to His Majesty King Charles III from all our students, families, and staff!"*

National Awareness

Schools need to use their position in the community to raise awareness of events relevant to their community for several reasons. By raising awareness of events such as Safer Internet Day, Black History Month, Armistice Day, Anti-Bullying Week, and International Day of Women and Girls in Science, schools can help to educate and inform their communities about important issues and topics. This can help to promote understanding, awareness, and action on these issues and can also serve as an opportunity for students to learn about and engage with the world around them.

By highlighting and celebrating the diversity of experiences and perspectives within the school community, schools can foster a positive and inclusive environment for all students, families, and staff. Promoting education, understanding, and awareness of relevant events can also help build a sense of community and belonging within the school. Here is a list of awareness days that may be relevant to schools and children in the UK:

- *Safer Internet Day: This annual event promotes online safety and helps to raise awareness of the risks and benefits of using the internet.*

- **Anti-Bullying Week**: *This annual event aims to raise awareness of the negative impact of bullying and to encourage actions to prevent bullying in schools and communities.*
- **Mental Health Awareness Week**: *This annual event aims to raise awareness of mental health and to promote the importance of good mental health for individuals and communities.*
- **National Children's Day UK**: *This annual event celebrates the rights and well-being of children and aims to raise awareness of the importance of supporting and protecting children's rights.*
- **International Day of the Girl**: *This annual event celebrates the rights and potential of girls and aims to raise awareness of the challenges and discrimination that girls face worldwide.*
- **World Autism Awareness Day**: *This annual event raises awareness of autism and promotes understanding and acceptance of individuals with autism.*
- **International Day of Persons with Disabilities**: *This annual event promotes the rights and well-being of persons with disabilities and aims to raise awareness of their challenges and barriers.*
- **International Day of Women and Girls in Science**: *This annual event celebrates the achievements and contributions of women and girls in science and aims to raise awareness of the importance of promoting gender equality in science, technology, engineering, and maths (STEM) fields.*

Examples of text for tweets could be:

- **Safer Internet Day**: *"Today is #SaferInternetDay! Let's all work together to create a safe and positive online environment for our students and communities. #OnlineSafety"*
- **Anti-Bullying Week**: *"It is #AntiBullyingWeek! Let's stand together and take action to create a safe and inclusive environment for all of our students. #StandUpForEachOther"*
- **Mental Health Awareness Week**: *"It is #MentalHealthAwarenessWeek! Let's prioritise the mental health and well-being of our students and communities.*

#MentalHealthMatters"
- ***National Children's Day UK****: "Happy #NationalChildrensDayUK! Let's celebrate the rights and well-being of all children and take action to support and protect their rights. #ChildrensRights"*
- ***International Day of the Girl****: "Happy #InternationalDayOfTheGirl! Let's celebrate the potential and achievements of girls and take action to promote gender equality and empower girls worldwide. #GirlPower"*
- ***World Autism Awareness Day****: "Today is #WorldAutismAwarenessDay! Let's raise awareness of autism and work towards creating a more inclusive and understanding society for individuals with autism. #LightItUpBlue"*
- ***International Day of Persons with Disabilities****: "Happy #InternationalDayOf PersonsWithDisabilities! Let's celebrate the achievements and contributions of individuals with disabilities and take action to promote their rights and well-being. #DisabilityRights"*
- ***International Day of Women and Girls in Science****: "Happy #InternationalDayO fWomenAndGirlsInScience! Let's celebrate the achievements and contributions of women and girls in science and take action to promote gender equality in STEM fields. #WomenInScience"*

The Zeitgeist

By posting information about trending issues in education, schools can help to keep their staff informed about the latest research, practices, and policies in the field. This can help promote professional development and support educators' ongoing learning and growth.

By engaging in discussions about current issues and challenges facing education, schools can help to foster a culture of critical thinking and problem-solving. They can support the efforts of educators to improve and innovate in their practice. Sharing information about trending education issues can also help foster a sense of community and collaboration within the school and the broader education community.

In addition to promoting professional development and collaboration, sharing information about trending issues in education can also help schools to provide thought leadership within the education community. By sharing research and insights about current education issues and challenges, schools can contribute to the ongoing conversation about best practices and innovations in the field. This can help position the school as a leader and an expert in the area and support the school's efforts to shape and influence education policy and practice.

Providing thought leadership through social media can also help schools to build their reputation and influence within the education community. By sharing valuable and insightful content, schools can demonstrate their expertise and establish themselves as trusted source of information and support for other educators.

Content Calendar

A content calendar can be a valuable tool for a school to plan and organise its social media posts in advance. There are several benefits to using a content calendar for school social media:

- *Consistency: A content calendar helps ensure that a school consistently posts high-quality content on social media. This can help build trust and engagement with followers.*
- *Efficiency: A content calendar allows a school to plan and schedule posts in advance, saving time and effort. This can be especially useful for busy school staff who may not have time to create new content on the fly constantly.*
- *Planning: A content calendar allows a school to plan out their content in advance, which can help ensure that they share a diverse range of relevant and engaging content with its audience.*

- **Collaboration**: *A content calendar can be a valuable tool for fostering co-operation among school staff. Different staff members can contribute ideas and suggestions for content, and the calendar can be used to coordinate and schedule posts.*

Using a content calendar can help a school effectively and efficiently plan and share content on social media, which can help build engagement and support for the school.

Conclusion

In conclusion, chapter ten discusses the various types of content schools can share on social media to engage and inform their community. This chapter also provides tips for crafting effective and engaging content and highlights the importance of considering the audience and platform when sharing content on social media. Schools can create a positive and inclusive online presence that aligns with their mission and values by identifying content pillars, only sharing content from trusted organisations, and celebrating religious holidays. It's important to remember that social media should be social, so don't forget to have fun and interact with your followers. Following these guidelines and remembering to have fun, schools can effectively use social media to promote their school, connect with their community, and create a positive online presence.

5

Social media tools for Schools

As a school, it is essential to use social media to increase brand awareness, recruit students and staff, and show leadership in the community. However, managing a successful social media strategy can be challenging, as it requires various skills, including graphic design, video production, copywriting, crisis management, analytics, and understanding current trends. It can be difficult for school leaders, teachers, and business managers to find the time and resources to execute a successful strategy, especially with the exponential advancement of social media. Poorly crafted posts can damage a school's brand, portraying it as amateurish. This chapter will discuss some of the top social media tools available to help schools streamline their efforts, produce high-quality content, and effectively manage their online presence. These tools can benefit schools that run their social media in-house, as they can save time and provide easy-to-use, affordable solutions. Alternatively, some schools outsource their social media management to companies like Social Media for Schools. Regardless of the approach taken, having access to practical social media tools is crucial for success in today's digital age.

Post Scheduling Software

Post-scheduling software can be a helpful tool for ensuring consistent and regular posting on social media. By scheduling posts in advance, you can avoid the stress of trying to create content at the last minute. There are many providers of post-scheduling software, but some of the best ones can be expensive and offer features that may be unnecessary for schools.

Post-scheduling can offer several benefits for schools, including ensuring consistent and regular posting, avoiding the stress of creating content at the last minute, and posting when staff may be unavailable. For example, scheduling posts during the half term can allow schools to continue sharing content and engaging with their audience even when staff are not in the office.

Scheduling posts can also help schools to optimize their content for different time zones and audiences. For example, if a school has many international followers, scheduling posts for optimal times in those time zones can help to increase engagement. Additionally, scheduling posts at specific times can help increase the visibility of content on social media platforms, as algorithms often prioritize content deemed most relevant to the user.

- ***Hootsuite*** *is a popular post-scheduling software that allows you to schedule posts on multiple social media platforms, including Facebook, Twitter, LinkedIn, and Instagram. It also offers analytics and social listening features to help you track the success of your content. However, it should be noted that its pricing plans can be steep, with the most expensive option costing around £475 per month. This may be too expensive for most schools, and the advanced features offered may not be necessary for their needs.*
- ***Buffer*** *is another popular post-scheduling software that offers similar features to Hootsuite, including scheduling for multiple social media platforms and analytics. It has a more affordable pricing structure but does not offer as many*

advanced features as Hootsuite.

Other post-scheduling software to consider include Sprout Social, Later, and Planoly. These tools offer a range of features, including scheduling, analytics, and social listening, but it should be noted that they can also be quite expensive. It is unlikely that schools will need all of the advanced features offered by these tools, so it is essential to carefully research the options available and choose the one that best fits your needs and budget.

Here are links to the post-scheduling software to get you started:

- *Hootsuite: https://hootsuite.com/*
- *Buffer: https://buffer.com/*
- *Sprout Social: https://www.sproutsocial.com/*
- *Later: https://www.later.com/*
- *Planoly: https://www.planoly*

Content Creation Software

Effective social media content creation is essential for schools looking to communicate effectively with their audience and promote their brand on social media. Consistently producing high-quality content can help schools stand out from the competition and engage their followers. However, it is necessary to note that poor-quality content can damage a school's brand and reputation.

Many tools and resources are available to help schools create compelling content for their social media channels. These can include:

- ***Graphic design*** *tools such as Canva (https://www.canva.com/) or Adobe*

Creative Cloud (https://www.adobe.com/creativecloud.html) allow schools to create visually appealing graphics, infographics, and other types of media.
- ***Video editing*** *tools such as Adobe Premiere (https://www.adobe.com/produ cts/premiere.html) or Final Cut Pro (https://www.apple.com/final-cut-pro/) can help schools create professional-quality videos to share on social media.*
- ***Writing and editing tools****, such as Grammarly (https://www.grammarly.com/) or ProWritingAid (https://prowritingaid.com/), can help schools ensure that their content is well-written and error-free.*

It should be noted that many of these tools can be expensive, and it may be more cost-effective for schools to use an agency like Social Media for Schools (https://www.socialmediaforschools.co.uk/), which uses these tools to create content for a large number of clients.

It is also vital for schools to have a content calendar in place to plan and organize their content creation efforts. This can help schools ensure that their content is consistent and aligned with their overall social media strategy.

Overall, social media content creation tools can be invaluable for schools looking to communicate effectively with their audience and promote their brand on social media. By investing in the right tools and resources, schools can create high-quality content that engages and inspires their followers while maintaining the integrity of their brand.

Royalty-Free Content

Although blurry pictures taken on the school's iPad can have a quaint charm... Using high-quality, professional images and other types of media can significantly improve the appearance of your social media content. However, it is essential to be mindful of copyright laws when using images and other media from the internet. Using images from Google or other search engines without proper permission can lead to copyright infringement, resulting in legal issues for your school.

To avoid this risk, it is recommended to use royalty-free content, which is content that is licensed for use without the need to pay royalties. Some many websites and resources offer royalty-free images and other media, including:

- **Pexels** *(https://www.pexels.com/)*
- **Unsplash** *(https://unsplash.com/)*
- **Pixabay** *(https://pixabay.com/)*
- **Shutterstock** *(https://www.shutterstock.com/)*

It is also worth noting that some social media platforms, such as Facebook and Instagram, offer libraries of royalty-free images that can be used in posts and ads. This can help schools create professional-looking social media content while maintaining the integrity of their brand. By using royalty-free content, schools can ensure that they are using high-quality images and other media without risking copyright infringement.

Conclusion

Choosing the right social media tools for your school can be daunting. With so many available options, it can be challenging to determine which ones fit your needs best. Many of the tools mentioned in this chapter offer free trials, which can be a helpful way to test them out and see which ones work best for your school.

However, it is essential to note that using social media effectively requires a well-thought-out strategy and a consistent, high-quality content calendar. For many schools, managing social media in-house can be time-consuming and resource-intensive, especially if you do not have staff with the necessary skills and experience.

In these cases, working with an agency like Social Media for Schools (https://www.socialmediaforschools.co.uk/) can be a valuable investment. Outsourcing your school's social media management to an agency can offer a range of benefits, including:

- **Price**: *Working with an agency can be more cost-effective than managing social media in-house, especially if you do not have staff with the necessary skills and experience. Social Media for Schools offers competitive pricing packages tailored to the needs of schools.*
- **Economies of scale**: *By partnering with an agency, schools can benefit from the economies of scale that come with managing social media for many clients. This can result in cost savings and access to advanced tools and resources that may not be available to individual schools.*
- **Time**: *Managing social media can be time-consuming, especially if you do not have a dedicated staff member. By outsourcing to an agency, schools can free up time and resources to focus on other priorities.*
- **Professionalism**: *Social Media for Schools is run by a qualified teacher and specialist leader of education, ensuring that the content created is professional and aligned with the needs of schools. By partnering with an agency, schools can ensure that their social media presence is professional and effective.*

In conclusion, outsourcing social media management to an agency like Social Media for Schools can be a valuable investment for schools looking to create a successful social media presence. By partnering with experienced professionals who understand the language of education and the importance of parental engagement, schools can ensure that their social media content is professional, effective, and aligned with their overall goals.

6

Build Your School's Social Media Audience

Social media can be a powerful tool for schools to engage with their communities and promote their brand. Building a solid and engaged audience on platforms such as Twitter, Facebook, and Instagram is essential for the success of a school's social media strategy. By regularly creating high-quality content that resonates with your audience and encourages them to engage with your school's social media channels, you can effectively promote your school's brand and values and build a solid and supportive community.

Social media can increase parental engagement, showcase the learning that takes place within the school, and highlight the values and ethos of the school. It can also be an effective tool for recruiting staff (Headworth, 2015) and attracting prospective parents.

However, it is vital to be aware of the potential risks associated with social media, such as negative reviews or comments from disgruntled school community members. A solid social media presence can help mitigate these risks by providing a platform for you to proactively communicate with your school community and address any concerns that may arise.

In this chapter, we will explore strategies for building a strong social media audience and maximising the impact of your school's social media presence. Whether you are just starting with social media or looking to improve your existing strategy, this chapter will provide you with the tools and techniques you need to succeed.

High-Quality Content

It is important to maintain momentum when posting, but they must also be of high quality. If they are not, it can damage your school's brand. Rich content is more likely to get 'shared' or 'retweeted' by existing followers and could potentially reach an entirely new audience of future followers (prospective parents)! It would be best if you aimed to share a range of content that aligns with your school's values and showcases the learning and achievements of your students.

According to research, the more positively a school (organisation) presents itself on social media, the more positively the public views the school (Sedalo G et al., 2022). By sharing high-quality content that promotes the values and achievements of your school, you can build a positive reputation and attract more followers.

Some ideas for content could include videos, graphics, questions, surveys, school information, or national holidays (and awareness days). Your school community is more likely to engage with posts they have a vested interest in, especially if their children are featured (policy permitting). Live streaming events or filming important information videos are ways to stand out from other schools.

Promote Relentlessly

It may seem obvious, but... **Promote, promote, promote**... and encourage everyone else to do the same. Be proactive in promoting your school's social media channels to ensure that you can reach and engage with as many members of your school community as possible. There are several ways to do this:

- *Include your social media handles on all correspondence, such as school newsletters and notice boards.*
- *Ask school and subject leaders to include links to your social media channels in their email signatures.*
- *Feature the "follow us" buttons along with your school website's Twitter, Facebook, and Instagram logos.*
- *Run competitions or challenges to encourage engagement on your social media channels. For example, you could ask classes to compete to see which one can get the most likes or shares on a particular post.*

By promoting your school's social media channels consistently and creatively, you can increase your followers and reach and, ultimately, build a stronger and more engaged community around your school.

Consistency

Posting consistently is essential for building a school's social media audience because it helps keep the school top of mind for your followers. When you post regularly, you are more likely to show up in your followers' feeds and be seen by them. This can help you build a strong and engaged audience over time. Here are practical tips for consistently posting high-quality content to assemble your school's social media audience:

- ***Plan ahead****: To ensure that you consistently post high-quality content, planning and scheduling your posts in advance can be helpful. This can help you stay organised and avoid gaps in your content calendar.*
- ***Use a content calendar****: A content calendar is a tool that helps you plan and organise your social media content. It can help you track what you have posted and what you have planned for the future.*
- ***Use a mix of content types****: To keep your followers engaged, try using a variety of content types, such as text posts, images, videos, polls, and more. This can help you reach a wider audience and keep your content fresh and exciting.*
- ***Use analytics to track your performance****: Many social media platforms have built-in analytics tools to help you track your posts' performance. Use these tools to see what types of content are performing well and adjust your strategy accordingly.*
- ***Seek feedback****: Ask your followers for feedback on your social media content. This can help you understand their likes and dislikes and give you ideas for future content.*
- ***Keep an eye on your competitors****: It can be helpful to see what other schools or organisations in your community are posting on social media. This can give you ideas for your content and help you stay competitive.*

Hashtags

Hashtags help your content get discovered by people who are interested in the same topics. When you include relevant hashtags in your posts, your content has a better chance of being seen by people searching for or following them.

For example, if your school hosts a science fair and you use the hashtag #sciencefair in your posts about the event, people interested in science fairs may come across your content when they search for or follow that hashtag. This can help you reach a wider audience and attract new followers who may not have otherwise discovered your content. Here are a few examples of hashtags that a school or teacher may use when posting on social media:

- *#education*
- *#teaching*
- *#studentsuccess*
- *#teachersofinstagram*
- *#teacherlife*
- *#studentlearning*
- *#classroom*
- *#teachergram*
- *#teachertools*
- *#teachersoftwitter*

These hashtags can reach a wider audience of educators and connect with other schools and teachers. Using relevant hashtags, schools and teachers can share their content with others interested in education and connect with like-minded individuals. It's also a good idea to use hashtags specific to your school or subject area, such as #[schoolname] or #[subjectname], to make it easier for people to find and connect with your content.

Engage with your School Community

Engaging with your followers is vital for building a school's social media audience because it helps build a sense of community and keeps your followers coming back for more. According to academic research, a strong sense of esprit de corps (or "team spirit") can have a positive impact on the success of an organisation (Berg, G., 2000). This is also true for schools, where a strong esprit de corps can help foster a sense of community and improve academic performance.

One way to build esprit de corps on social media is by engaging with your followers. By responding to comments and questions and encouraging interaction with your school's social media accounts, you can create a more personal and interactive experience for your followers. This can help foster a sense of belonging and encourage more engagement with your school.

In addition to engaging with your followers, you can also build esprit de corps by sharing user-generated content and highlighting the achievements and successes of your students and faculty. This can help create a sense of pride and accomplishment within your school community and strengthen the bond between members.

Overall, building esprit de corps on social media is vital for creating a strong and engaged community for your school. By fostering a sense of community and highlighting your students' and faculty' achievements and successes, you can create a positive and supportive environment that helps drive academic and organisational success.

Stop! Collaborate and Listen...

According to academic research, collaborating with other schools and organisations can effectively build a school's social media audience. This is especially true when partnering with teacher social media influencers or businesses with a solid corporate social responsibility (CSR) focus (van Schaik, 2022).

Teacher social media influencers, or educators with a large and engaged following on social media, can help promote your school's content and attract new followers (Carpenter et al., 2022). By collaborating with these influencers, you can tap into their audience and potentially reach a new group interested in your school community.

Similarly, businesses with a strong focus on CSR can also be valuable partners for schools. By collaborating with these businesses, schools can showcase their commitment to social and environmental issues and potentially attract new followers who are interested in similar causes.

Collaborating with other schools, teacher social media influencers, and businesses with a strong CSR focus can effectively build a school's social media audience. These partnerships can help you reach a wider audience, establish relationships, and demonstrate your commitment to important causes.

Paid Advertising

Using paid social media advertising can be an effective way to build a school's social media audience. Still, it requires a deep understanding of social media algorithms and best practices and a clear strategy for reaching your desired audience. To ensure that your ad campaign is successful and helps you achieve your goals, working with professionals with experience in social media advertising for schools may be beneficial.

These professionals understand schools' unique needs and goals and can help create a targeted and effective ad campaign that reaches the right audience. They can also help you avoid common pitfalls and ensure that your ad budget is used effectively.

Overall, working with professionals with experience in social media advertising for schools can be an invaluable resource for building your school's social media audience. By leveraging their expertise and understanding of the unique needs of schools, you can create an effective ad campaign that helps you reach your goals and grow your audience.

Conclusion

In conclusion, building a strong social media audience is essential for the success of a school's online presence. By regularly posting high-quality content, engaging with your followers, and collaborating with other schools and organisations, you can create a positive and supportive community around your school. Additionally, paid social media advertising and working with professionals who understand the unique needs of schools can be effective strategies for building your school's social media audience. By following these strategies and being proactive in promoting your school's social media channels, you can build a strong and engaged audience that supports your school's goals and values.

7

Make your School's social media Stand Out

This chapter will explore strategies for making your school's social media stand out above the rest. With the increasing use of social media by schools, it is vital to have a strong and engaging online presence that sets your school apart from others. By following best practices and using innovative techniques, you can create a social media presence that showcases your school's unique values and attracts a loyal and engaged audience.

Whether you are just starting with social media or looking to improve your existing strategy, this chapter will provide the tools and techniques you need to create a standout social media presence for your school.

School Values and Ethos

Communicating your school's values and ethos to the wider community is essential, and social media is a quick and effective way to do so. Ofsted, the UK's education inspection body, says that the values and ethos of a school are the foundations of its work and that they can help to create a positive culture in which pupils can thrive and achieve their best (Ofsted, 2022).

The Department for Education (DfE) similarly emphasises the importance of a school's values and ethos, stating that they contribute to the overall quality of education and pupils' spiritual, moral, cultural, mental and physical development (Department for Education, 2014).

While school websites may contain detailed explanations of values, they may not always be easily accessible or actively sought out by readers. In contrast, social media platforms are easily accessible and can reach a wider audience, including parents who may not visit the school website. By sharing your school's values on social media, you can create a unique identity for your school and differentiate it from others.

By actively sharing your school's values on social media, you can demonstrate your commitment to creating a positive and inclusive school community, as encouraged by both Ofsted and the DfE.

A Window into the Classrooms

One of the most effective ways to engage parents and other school community members is by sharing photos and videos of the exciting learning experiences in your classrooms. This helps to bridge the communication gap between home and school and allows parents to feel connected to their child's education. Sharing images of students showcasing their schoolwork also sends a positive message that they are valued and celebrated, which can be particularly appealing to prospective parents.

Examples of things teachers could share on social media include photos of students working on projects, videos of presentations or performances, and updates on field trips or other special events. The Education Endowment Foundation (EEF) recommends using social media to "share learning resources, photos and videos of student's work, and information about after-school clubs and other extra-curricular activities" (EEF, 2021). This can help to create a sense of community and involvement for parents and can also help to showcase the quality of education and opportunities available at your school.

According to Hosen et al. (2021), parents play a vital role in supporting their child's learning and are critical partners in their education. By sharing updates and information on social media, teachers can help keep parents informed and involved in their child's education, which can positively impact student achievement.

By leveraging the power of social media, schools can create a more connected and supportive learning environment for students. In contrast, a school that does not use social media to share updates and information may struggle to engage and involve parents in their child's education. This could lead to a lack of communication and understanding between home and school, negatively impacting student learning and achievement.

Your School's Newsletter

The weekly school newsletter can sometimes be a bit uninspiring. Why not share shorter weekly posts to drip-feed the information whilst creating a strong social media presence?

These posts need not be onerous to create but should be informative. They can be helpful with content such as upcoming events, job vacancies, and key dates. Doing this will undoubtedly increase your following because no parent will want to miss out. This type of organic engagement will make your school stand out.

While school newsletters can be a helpful way to communicate important information to parents and other members of the school community, they may not always capture everyone's attention. One way to increase engagement and create a more substantial social media presence is by sharing shorter posts throughout the week, which can help your audience by drip-feeding information.

These posts do not need to be time-consuming to create but should be informative and provide valuable information to parents, such as upcoming events, job vacancies, and key dates. By sharing this type of content on social media, you can help to ensure that no parent misses out on important updates and events.

In contrast, a school that does not use social media to share information and updates regularly may struggle to communicate effectively with parents and other school community members. By leveraging the power of social media, schools can create a more connected and supportive learning environment for students.

In addition to increasing engagement and building a strong social media presence, this approach can help make your school stand out. By using social media to share information and updates with parents actively, you can demonstrate your commitment to transparency and communication, which can be appealing to prospective parents and other members of the school community.

Establishing Thought Leadership

To make your school stand out, it is good to be seen as a school actively seeking a broader perspective on important issues. Social media provides a platform for teachers and schools to connect with and learn from other educational establishments and organisations. By participating in discussions and sharing best practices, schools can become thought leaders in their field and make their schools stand out.

Thought leadership refers to consistently producing and sharing valuable and innovative ideas, insights, and perspectives that inspire and inform others (Lorange, 2021). In the education sector, thought leadership can involve sharing research, resources, and best practices on social media, as well as engaging in discussions and debates about important issues in education. By actively participating in these conversations, schools can establish themselves as leaders in their field and contribute to the wider conversation about education.

In addition to establishing thought leadership, participating in discussions and sharing best practices on social media can also support professional development and continuous improvement. By staying up to date with the latest research and approaches in education, teachers can enhance their skills and knowledge, ultimately benefiting their students.

According to research by Saldañaet al. l (2021), teachers and schools can use social media to become influencers in their fields, sharing their knowledge, experiences and insights with their followers. By actively tracking and using relevant hashtags on Twitter, schools can access a wealth of resources and perspectives on important issues in education. This can help broaden the scope of learning and development opportunities for teachers and students.

In addition to seeking out new insights and perspectives, schools can also use social media to share their knowledge and experiences with others. Schools can become go-to sources of information and inspiration for fellow educators by engaging in discussions and sharing content on platforms like Twitter.

By leveraging the power of social media, schools can create a more connected and collaborative learning environment that promotes thought leadership, professional development, and continuous improvement.

Global Experiences for Your Students

Social media allows students to connect and participate in global experiences with their peers worldwide. By leveraging the power of social media, schools can create unique learning opportunities for their students that may not be possible through traditional methods.

Global experiences, including cultural exchange and immersion programs, can positively impact students' academic and personal development. Research suggests that students who participate in international exchange programs or other global experiences show improved critical thinking skills, problem-solving abilities, and cross-cultural competence (Cullinan, 2022). In addition, cultural backgrounds can help students develop empathy, understanding, and respect for others, which are critical skills in today's globalised world (Turing Scheme, 2020).

There are many ways that schools can facilitate global experiences and interactions for their students through social media. For example, schools can use platforms like Skype or Zoom to connect with schools in other countries for virtual cultural exchange programs. Students can also participate in online language learning programs or engage in cultural exchange through pen pal programs or social media groups focused on language and cultural exchange.

Of course, it is vital to prioritise online safety and safeguard children while participating in these activities. This can be done through internet safety lessons and by adhering to the school's internet safety policy. Schools can also start by facilitating communication with other classes within the school as a way for students to become familiar with safe interactions on social media.

By providing opportunities for global experiences and interactions through social media, schools can make their school stand out and create a more connected and diverse learning environment for their students.

Best Times to post

Optimising the times you post on social media can help schools to increase the visibility and reach of their content. Different social media platforms have different user demographics and usage patterns, so schools must consider the best times to post based on their target audience and platform.

Many social media scheduling tools, such as Hootsuite and Buffer, offer the option to schedule posts at the optimal times based on the school's specific followers. This can effectively ensure that content is being posted at the best times for maximum engagement and reach.

For example, our evidence-informed (Kordzadeh, 2022) experience has shown that the best times for schools to post on Facebook are during the weekdays, with the highest engagement occurring on Thursdays and Fridays. On Twitter, the best times for schools to post are during the weekdays, with the highest engagement occurring midweek and during the lunch hour. On Instagram, the best times for schools to post are during the weekdays, with the highest engagement occurring on Wednesdays.

By posting at the optimal times, schools can increase the chances that their target audiences will see their content and potentially generate more engagement (likes, comments, shares, etc.). This can help build the school's online presence and reach and support its overall social media marketing efforts.

Conclusion

In conclusion, social media is a powerful tool that can help schools promote their values and ethos, engage with parents and other school community members, share information and updates, and connect with other educational establishments and organisations. By leveraging the power of social media, schools can create a standout online presence that sets them apart from others. They can also support professional development, thought leadership, and continuous improvement. By following best practices and using innovative techniques, schools can create a social media presence that is engaging, informative, and inclusive and helps build a solid and supportive school community. Here are some main takeaways from this chapter:

- *Social media effectively promotes your school's values and ethos and creates a unique identity.*
- *Sharing photos and videos of students' learning experiences on social media can help to bridge the home-school communication gap and engage parents.*
- *Virtual tours can be a powerful way to showcase your school to prospective parents.*
- *Drip-feeding your school newsletter content through social media can help to increase your following and keep parents informed.*
- *Participating in discussions and sharing best practices on social media can support thought leadership and professional development.*
- *Social media can facilitate global experiences and interactions for students, such as connecting with pen pals in other countries.*
- *Optimising the times you post on social media can help increase your content's visibility and reach.*
- *Scheduling tools can help identify the best times to post based on your followers.*
- *Thoughtful and strategic use of social media can help schools to create a standout online presence and build a solid and supportive school community.*

8

Social Media Policies for Schools

As social media becomes increasingly prevalent in schools, schools need clear guidelines on how staff, students, and parents should use social networking sites. These social media policies protect the school community, particularly children and ensure that the appropriate protocols are in place for the proper use of social media.

It is natural for students, parents, and staff to want to share special moments and events from school on social media, such as class assemblies, school plays, and sports days. However, it is essential to have guidelines in place to ensure that these posts are respectful and appropriate and that the privacy and safety of the school community are protected.

In this chapter, we will explore the purpose and benefits of social media policies in schools and provide guidance on developing and implementing adequate procedures. We will also discuss the potential risks and challenges of social media use and offer strategies for managing these risks in a way that promotes a safe and supportive school community.

Do Schools need a social media policy?

The law does not require schools to have a specific social media policy in the United Kingdom. However, schools are expected to follow relevant legal and regulatory guidelines when using social media, such as those related to data protection and safeguarding.

It is generally advisable for schools to have a clear and comprehensive social media policy in place to guide the appropriate use of social media by staff, students, and parents. This can help to ensure that the school is meeting its legal and regulatory obligations and can also help to prevent potential risks and challenges associated with social media use.

Having a social media policy can also provide a framework for the school to communicate its expectations and guidelines for social media use and can help to promote a safe and supportive school community. Schools may wish to consult with their local authority or governing body for guidance on developing a social media policy that is appropriate for their school.

Often, these policies are split into three clear sections directed at staff, parents, and pupils.

Typical Guidelines for Staff

There are several best practices that school staff should follow when using social media to ensure that they are acting in the best interests of the school and its students. These include:

- ***Not accepting friend requests from current or former pupils****: This can help* *to maintain appropriate boundaries and prevent potential issues related to confidentiality and professionalism.*

- **Informing the parents and school leaders if a child sends a friend request**: *This can help ensure appropriate communication and transparency in these situations.*
- **Refraining from discussing school-related matters or posting photos of school events on personal social media pages**: *This can help protect the school community's privacy and confidentiality and ensure that staff act professionally.*
- **Not identifying themselves as being associated with the school on personal social media**: *This can help prevent potential conflicts of interest and ensure that staff can maintain a personal online presence separate from their professional role.*
- **Using the tightest privacy settings can help** *protect personal information and prevent unauthorised access to personal social media accounts.*
- **Refraining from using personal social media on school devices**: *This can help to ensure that school devices are being used for appropriate purposes and prevent potential issues related to security and confidentiality.*

By following these best practices, school staff can use social media in a respectful, responsible, and professional way that promotes the best interests of the school and its students.

Typical Guidelines for Parents

Parents should follow several best practices when using social media to ensure that they are acting in the best interests of the school and its students. These include:

- **Avoid posting photos, videos, or comments that include other children at the school**: *This can help protect the school community's privacy and* *confidentiality and ensure that children's images are not shared without their or their parent's consent.*

- **Only using the school's formal communication channels for queries, concerns, and complaints can help** *ensure that communication is timely and appropriate and that problems are addressed formally and professionally.*
- **Refraining from posting anything malicious about the school or any member of the school community**: *This can help to promote a positive and supportive school community and prevent potential issues related to reputation and relationships.*

By following these best practices, parents can use social media in a way that is respectful, responsible, and supportive of the school and its students.

Typical Guidelines for Children

There are several best practices that pupils should follow when using social media to ensure that they act in the school's best interests and themselves. These include:

- **Not joining any social networking sites if they are below the permitted age (13 for most sites, including Facebook and Instagram)**: *This can help ensure that children comply with legal and regulatory requirements and are protected from potential risks and associated challenges with social media use.*
- **Informing their parents if they are using social networking sites**: *This can help to ensure that there is appropriate communication and oversight and that parents are aware of their child's online activities.*
- **Awareness of how to report abuse and inappropriate content**: *This can help ensure that children can protect themselves and others from harm and act if they encounter inappropriate or harmful content online.*
- **Refraining from making inappropriate comments (including in private messages) about the school, teachers, or other children**: *This can help to*

promote a positive and respectful school community and prevent potential issues related to reputation and relationships.

- ***Not sharing personal information, such as their full name, address, phone number, or date of birth****: This can help to protect their privacy and prevent potential risks such as identity theft or stalking.*
- ***Being cautious about accepting friend requests from strangers can help*** *protect their safety and prevent potential risks such as online bullying or grooming.*
- ***Using strong and unique passwords for their social media accounts can help*** *protect their accounts from unauthorised access and prevent potential risks such as hacking or identity theft.*
- ***Seeking help from a trusted adult if they encounter any issues or problems online****: This can help to ensure that they have support and guidance in addressing any challenges or concerns that may arise.*
- ***Using privacy settings to control who can see their posts and personal information****: This can help to protect their privacy and control who has access to their online content.*
- ***Being mindful of their online reputation and the potential long-term consequences of their actions****: This can help ensure that they are making responsible and respectful choices and considering the impact of their online activities on their prospects.*

By following these best practices, pupils can use social media in a safe, responsible, and respectful way that promotes the best interests of the school and themselves.

Social Media Screening Policy

It is vital to screen the social media of people who work with children to ensure that they are suitable to work with children, protect the school's reputation, and safeguard the children. By conducting social media screening, schools can identify any potential safeguarding risks posed by prospective candidates, such as evidence of inappropriate behaviour or comments or any behaviour that could potentially harm the children in their care (Department for Education, 2022).

Conducting social media screening for schools can be a complex and potentially risky process. It is essential for school leaders to be aware of the potential dangers and challenges associated with this process and to take steps to minimise any potential risks.

One potential danger is the risk of violating employment and discrimination laws. School leaders must avoid using protected characteristics (such as age, ethnicity, religion, health, sexual orientation, and family life) as part of their decision-making process. It is also important to obtain consent from candidates before accessing their social media profiles, as this can be seen as an invasion of privacy.

Another potential danger is the risk of making judgments based on unconscious bias. School leaders may unknowingly form conclusions based on biased or incomplete information by relying on social media profiles to assess candidates. This can lead to unfair or incorrect decisions and may result in the school missing out on talented candidates (James, 2022)

There is also the risk of accessing the wrong person's social media profile or collecting and using data violating data protection laws. To avoid these risks, school leaders may consider using a professional social media screening service, such as Social Media For Schools Screening. This service can help to accurately assess the potential safeguarding risks posed by candidates while protecting the school's reputation and leaders from possible legal liabilities.

By using an organisation like Social Media for Schools to conduct your screening, you are outsourcing to an organisation on your side – our core business is to protect and elevate schools' reputations. We will also show you and the candidate the professional courtesy that teaching and working in schools deserves.

Conclusion

In conclusion, social media policies are an essential tool for schools to ensure that the appropriate protocols are in place for the proper use of social media. Schools should consider developing and implementing clear social media policies that outline expectations and guidelines for staff, students, and parents. These policies can help protect the school community, particularly children, and ensure that social media is used responsibly and professionally.

Some key takeaways to consider when developing social media policies for your school include the following:

- *Guiding on the appropriate use of social media for staff, students, and parents*
- *Implementing clear consequences for any breaches of the social media policy*
- *Regularly reviewing and updating the social media policy to ensure it is practical and relevant.*
- *Obtaining consent for social media screening*
- *Managing unconscious bias when reviewing social media profiles*
- *Ensuring that you are checking the correct social media profile*
- *Protecting personal data and adhering to data protection laws*

9

Handling Criticism on social media

Although 99% of interactions on school social media pages are positive, it would be foolish to ignore the impact of negative interactions. The effects they can have on the reputation of the school and the morale of the school community can be far-reaching. Schools must maintain a healthy online presence to reap the benefits of improved parental engagement, increased school brand awareness, and taking their place in a global school community. They also need to know how to deal with criticism, negativity, and in the worst cases... false allegations.

While it is natural to want to avoid negative feedback, it is essential to remember that handling criticism and complaints professionally and constructively can help build trust and improve your school's reputation.

According to research, social media has become an increasingly popular platform for individuals to voice their complaints or concerns about businesses, organisations, and public institutions (Appel et al., 2020). This includes schools. While it may not be the most pleasant experience, dealing with criticism and complaints on social media can provide an opportunity for your school to address any issues and improve the experience of your students and families.

This chapter will explore strategies for handling criticism and complaints about your school on social media. We will discuss the importance of listening to feedback, responding promptly and professionally, and using criticism as an opportunity for improvement. By following these best practices, you can effectively manage negative feedback on social media and maintain a positive online presence for your school.

Negative comment received

While it may be tempting to delete negative comments or reviews on your school's social media, research suggests this can worsen the situation. According to a study published in the Journal of Consumer Behaviour, deleting negative comments can lead to higher levels of perceived censorship and a decline in trust from the community (Nikbin, 2022). This is because deleting negative comments can be perceived as an attempt to cover up the issue or avoid accountability rather than addressing the concerns or criticisms raised.

Instead of deleting negative comments, it is generally better to address and resolve the issue constructively. This can help to build trust and credibility with your school community and can also help to prevent similar problems from arising in the future.

Assess the situation

Take a moment to assess the situation before responding to negative comments on social media. This can help to ensure that you are responding in a calm and measured manner rather than reacting impulsively. When assessing the situation, consider the following factors:

· ***The severity of the issue**: Is the negative comment simply a complaint or criticism, or is it a more serious issue that requires immediate attention? If the* *problem is more serious, such as a threat to the safety or well-being of your school community, it may be necessary to address it immediately.*

- **The context of the comment**: *Consider the context in which the negative comment was made. Was it created in response to a specific post or event, or was it a more general criticism of your school? Understanding the context can help you to craft a more targeted and effective response.*
- **The tone of the comment**: *Pay attention to the style of the comment and try to determine the underlying emotion behind it. Is the commenter angry, frustrated, or upset? Understanding the sentiment behind the comment can help you to craft a more empathetic and understanding response.*
- **The audience of the comment**: *Consider the potential audience of the comment. Is it visible to a broad audience, or is it limited to a small group of people? Understanding the comment's possible reach can help you determine the appropriate response.*

It is important to remember that not every negative comment requires immediate attention, and it may be appropriate to wait until a later time to address specific issues. However, if the problem is more severe or needs immediate attention, it is essential to take timely and appropriate action.

Calm and Considered

It is important to remember that responding to negative comments on social media calmly and respectfully is crucial. While it may be tempting to become defensive or emotional, it is essential to remember that the goal is to resolve the issue and maintain the school's reputation. By crafting a professional and measured response, you can help defuse the situation and demonstrate to all readers, including pupils and colleagues, how to handle negative feedback rationally and maturely.

Take offline

Schools should have a plan to handle negative comments on their social media platforms. According to research, deleting negative comments can often escalate the situation and lead to further negative feedback (Kim et al., 2015). Instead, schools should take a calm and considerate approach to responding to negative comments.

One way to diffuse the situation is to take the conversation off the school's social media platform and continue it privately (Kim et al., 2015). This allows the school to address the issue without engaging in a public discussion that could escalate the situation further. This should be written as a response on the post so that other members of the community can see that you are addressing the situation but that it is not a conversation that needs to be public. You do not want yourself or staff members embroiled in a public discussion. This could become inflammatory and result in more damage than good.

Gather Evidence

Suppose you become aware of any information or allegations damaging towards a staff member or the school. It is essential to gather evidence when dealing with negative comments or allegations on social media to establish the facts of the situation. This evidence can be used to support any ongoing complaints or cases and can help to determine the appropriate course of action.

To gather evidence effectively, it is paramount to:

- *Take screenshots of the comments or posts in question, including the time and date of the incident.*
- *Record the username of the individual who made a comment or post.*
- *Create a chronology of events to provide context and help understand the sequence of events.*

- *If the comments or posts are made in a closed group, try to gather information on the group administrator in case further action is needed.*

Remember to respect the privacy and confidentiality of individuals involved and only gather the relevant and necessary evidence to the situation. Using this evidence fairly and objectively can help to support your school and protect its reputation.

Mental Health and Well being

School leaders have a duty of care to protect their staff and pupils from third-party harassment. The level of support required will be down to the individual. However, it is essential to remember that negative comments and criticism on social media can significantly impact the mental health and well-being of those affected. School leaders must provide support and resources to staff and students who may be experiencing distress because of such comments. This could include offering counselling services, providing access to mental health resources, or simply creating a safe and supportive environment where individuals can share their experiences and emotions. Staff may also want to contact their union or other organisations. This is especially important if legal advice is required for allegations or accusations.

Additionally, it is essential to address the root cause of negative comments and complaints, whether they are related to school policies, staff behaviour, or other issues. By addressing these underlying issues and creating a positive and inclusive school culture, school leaders can help prevent future negative comments and criticism on social media.

Be Proactive.

Schools can proactively take several steps to manage the risk of criticism and unfounded allegations proactively. One important measure is to have a dedicated Social Media Manager responsible for monitoring comments and activity on the school's social media platforms. Monitoring tools and apps can also help identify negative comments or unsavoury activity on the school's accounts before they become widely visible.

In addition to monitoring activity on social media, you should have clear policies to address potentially hostile situations. This includes an Acceptable User Policy that sets out expectations for staff and students' safe and responsible use of digital technology and the internet. This policy should be signed by all staff and students and should outline the consequences of any breaches. Schools can also ask parents to support this effort by monitoring their children's use of social media when they are not in school.

Establishing policies can provide structure and clarity in potentially tricky situations. Including a social media section in the school's Complaints Policy is also helpful. This way, there is a straightforward procedure to follow if an online allegation is made against the school. Overall, being proactive and having clear policies and procedures in place can help schools to minimise the risk of criticism and unfounded allegations.

Parental Voice.

Schools can try setting up a parents' forum where parents can share their thoughts and feedback in a safe and respectful environment to give parents a voice and reduce the risk of negative comments on social media. Encouraging open communication and active listening to parent concerns can help to build a sense of community and prevent negative comments from being posted online.

In addition to creating a positive environment for communication, schools can also work to foster a whole school understanding of how to use social media respectfully. This can involve engaging parents and educating them on how they can contribute to the school's efforts to create a positive culture around social media use. Regularly sharing content about student achievements and positive experiences can help to build a sense of community and reduce the temptation for parents to post negative comments.

By giving parents a voice and creating a positive culture around social media use, schools can help reduce the risk of negative comments and online rants. Embedding safe social media use in the curriculum through lessons on Internet Safety, PSHE, and Computing can also help to educate students and parents about the responsible use of social media. Additionally, providing information and resources to parents about social media use can be helpful, as some parents may be new to these platforms.

Outsource Your social media

Outsourcing your school's social media management to a specialised company can have several benefits when dealing with negative comments or trolling. One of the main advantages is that it creates an extra layer of protection between your school's staff and potentially harmful or inflammatory comments. Trolls often seek to elicit an emotional response from their words. By outsourcing your social media management to a company trained to handle these situations, you can prevent staff members from reacting impulsively and potentially making a rash decision.

This extra "barrier" can also discourage trolls from commenting in the first place, as they may be less likely to receive the emotional response they desire. Additionally, outsourcing your social media management to a specialised company can ensure that your school's social media presence is well-managed and maintained, even during times of high stress or negative comments.

Overall, outsourcing your school's social media management can help to protect your staff and effectively manage negative comments while also allowing you to focus on other essential tasks.

Conclusion

In conclusion, chapter nine addressed handling criticism on social media, a common challenge for schools. Schools need to have a plan to respond to negative comments, as they can impact the school's reputation and the well-being of staff and students. When faced with negative comments, schools must assess the situation, remain calm and considerate in their response, and take the conversation offline if necessary. Gathering evidence can also help address the issue and determine the best course of action. It is also essential for schools to consider the mental health and well-being of their staff and students when responding to criticism on social media.

Key takeaways from this chapter include:

- *The importance of having a plan in place for responding to negative comments on social media.*
- *The need to remain calm and considered in the face of criticism.*
- *The role of mental health and well-being in handling criticism on social media.*

10

Online Safety

Online safety has been a consistent theme throughout this book, as it is an essential aspect of social media use for schools and teachers. As noted in research by Mirra (2022), schools and teachers are important role models for their students and can influence how students think about and use social media. By role-modelling online safety through the school's social media channels, schools and teachers can show students how to use these platforms positively and respectfully.

In addition to promoting online safety, effectively role-modelling good behaviour on social media can also help students develop crucial digital citizenship skills, such as empathy, respect, and responsibility (Oh, 2022). These skills are essential for navigating the digital world and building positive online communities.

As the Minister for Digital and Tech Economy & Online Safety, Damian Collins MP, stated:

> *"It is important that we ensure that children are protected online and that they are aware of the risks and consequences of their actions. It is our responsibility to educate young people about how to use the internet safely and responsibly and to provide them with the tools and resources*

they need to navigate the digital world. Social Media platforms also have a responsibility to ensure that they aren't allowing children to access harmful content and not actively promoting harmful content to children."
(Collins, 2022)

By teaching students about the importance of digital citizenship and the responsibilities of social media platforms, schools and teachers can help students become engaged, responsible and respectful members of the online community.

11

Conclusion

Social media can be a powerful tool for schools to connect with their community, promote their school, and engage with students and families. In this book, "Social Media for Schools," we have explored the benefits and best practices for using social media in educational settings. From getting started with social media to handling criticism and promoting online safety, this book has attempted to provide valuable insights and ideas for creating a successful online presence based on our experience looking after the social media accounts for numerous schools, colleges and universities.

Throughout the book, we have examined how schools can use social media to engage with their audience, including promoting school events and achievements, sharing resources and educational tips, and building a positive and engaging narrative. We have also discussed the importance of setting strategic aims, creating an audience, and maintaining a consistent presence on social media.

In addition to these strategies, we have also addressed the challenges that schools may face when using social media, including managing negative comments, promoting online safety, and developing social media policies.

Following the guidelines outlined in this book, schools can effectively use social media to connect with their community and create a positive online presence.

References

Appel, G., Grewal, L., Hadi, R. and Stephen, A.T., 2020. The future of social media in marketing. Journal of the Academy of Marketing Science, 48(1), pp.79-95.

Berg, G., 2000. School culture and teachers' Esprit de Corps. Balázs, É., Wieringen v. F., Watson, L.: Quality and educational management. Budapest, Mueszaki Koenykiadó, pp.49-77.

Bruguera, C., Guitert, M. and Romeu, T., 2019. Social media and professional development: A systematic review. Research in Learning Technology, 27.

Carpenter, J.P., Shelton, C.C. and Schroeder, S.E., 2022. The education influencer: A new player in the educator professional landscape. Journal of Research on Technology in Education, pp.1-16.

Collins MP, D. (2022). Switched on? How technology is transforming our way of life.

Cullinan, J., Flannery, D. and Palcic, D., 2022. Study abroad programme participation and subsequent academic performance: evidence from administrative data. Education Economics, 30(3), pp.251-269.

Department for Education (2014). Promoting fundamental British values through SMSC. [online] GOV.UK. Available at: https://www.gov.uk/government/publications/promoting-fundamental-british-values-through-smsc [Accessed 29 Dec. 2022].

Department for Education (2021). *Education and training statistics for the UK, Reporting Year 2021.* [online] Department for Education. Available at: https://expl ore-education-statistics.service.gov.uk/find-statistics/education-and-training-st atistics-for-the-uk [Accessed 29 Dec. 2022].

Department for Education (2022). *Keeping children safe in education.* [online] GOV.UK. Available at: https://www.gov.uk/government/publications/keeping-chil dren-safe-in-education—2 [Accessed 29 Dec. 2022].

Duggan, M., Lenhart, A., Lampe, C. and Ellison, N.B., 2015. *Parents and social media. Pew Research Center,* 16(1), p.2.

Education Endowment Foundation. (2021). *Parental Engagement.* [online] Available at: https://educationendowmentfoundation.org.uk/education-evide nce/teaching-learning-toolkit/parental-engagement [Accessed 29 Dec. 2022].

Farrell, A.F. and Collier, M.A., 2010. *School personnel's perceptions of family-school communication: A qualitative study. Improving Schools,* 13(1), pp.4-20.

Hayes, B., James, A., Barn, R. and Watling, D., 2022. *"The world we live in now": A qualitative investigation into parents', teachers', and children's perceptions of social networking site use. British Journal of Educational Psychology,* 92(1), pp.340-363.

Headworth, A., 2015. *Social media recruitment: How to successfully integrate social media into recruitment strategy. Kogan Page Publishers.*

Hoover-Dempsey, K.V. and Sandler, H.M., 1995. *Parental involvement in children's education: Why does it make a difference? Teachers college record,* 97(2), pp.310-331.

Hosen, M., Ogbeibu, S., Giridharan, B., Cham, T.H., Lim, W.M. and Paul, J., 2021. *Individual motivation and social media influence on student knowledge sharing* and learning performance: Evidence from an emerging economy. *Computers & Education*, 172, p.104262.

James, S. (2022). *Social Media Screening for Schools.* [online] Social Media for Schools. Available at: https://socialmediaforschools.co.uk/social-media-screening-for-schools/ [Accessed 29 Dec. 2022].

Johnson, K. (2020). *5 ways to develop a long-term strategy for diversity, equity & inclusion on social media.* [online] Sprout Social. Available at: https://sproutsocial.com/insights/brand-diversity-in-social-media/ [Accessed 29 Dec. 2022].

Jones, K. (2021). *Council Post: The Importance Of Branding In Business.* [online] Forbes. Available at: https://www.forbes.com/sites/forbesagencycouncil/2021/03/24/the-importance-of-branding-in-business [Accessed 29 Dec. 2022].

Kim, W.G., Lim, H. and Brymer, R.A., 2015. *The effectiveness of managing social media on hotel performance. International Journal of Hospitality Management*, 44, pp.165–171.

Kordzadeh, N. and Young, D.K., 2022. *How social media analytics can inform content strategies. Journal of Computer Information Systems*, 62(1), pp.128–140.

Lorange, P., 2008. *Thought leadership meets business: How business schools can become more successful. Cambridge University Press.*

McCausland, A. (2020). *Why branding is important for your school (and even more important right now).* [online] Elevate Creative. Available at: https://elevatecreative.com.au/why-branding-is-important-for-your-school/ [Accessed 29 Dec. 2022].

Mirra, N., McGrew, S., Kahne, J., Garcia, A. and Tynes, B., 2022. *Expanding digital citizenship education to address tough issues. Phi Delta Kappan*, 103(5), pp.31–35.

Nikbin, D., Aramo, T., Iranmanesh, M. and Ghobakhloo, M., 2022. *Impact of brands' Facebook page characteristics and followers' comments on trust building and purchase intention: Alternative attractiveness as moderator. Journal of Consumer Behaviour, 21(3), pp.494-508.*

NSPCC (2021). *Online safety. [online] NSPCC. Available at: https://www.nspcc.org.uk/keeping-children-safe/online-safety/ [Accessed 29 Dec. 2022].*

Office for National Statistics (2020). *Internet access – households and individuals, Great Britain – Office for National Statistics. [online] www.ons.gov.uk. Available at: https://www.ons.gov.uk/peoplepopulationandcommunity/householdcharacteristics/homeinternetandsocialmediausage/bulletins/internetaccesshouseholdsandindividuals/2020 [Accessed 29 Dec. 2022].*

Ofsted (2022). *School Inspection handbook. [online] GOV.UK. Available at: https://www.gov.uk/government/publications/school-inspection-handbook-eif/school-inspection-handbook [Accessed 29 Dec. 2022].*

Oh, C., Carducci, B., Vaivada, T. and Bhutta, Z.A., 2022. *Interventions to promote physical activity and healthy digital media use in children and adolescents: a systematic review. Pediatrics, 149(Supplement 6).*

Rim, H. and Song, D., 2016. *"How negative becomes less negative": Understanding the effects of comment valence and response sidedness in social media. Journal of communication, 66(3), pp.475-495.*

Saldaña, C.M., Welner, K., Malcolm, S. and Tisch, E., 2021. *Teachers as market influencers: Towards a policy framework for teacher brand ambassador programs in K-12 schools. Education Policy Analysis Archives, 29(August-December).*

Sedalo, G., Boateng, H. and Kosiba, J.P., 2022. *Exploring social media affordance in relationship marketing practices in SMEs. Digital Business, 2(1), p.100017.*

Turing Scheme. (n.d.). Turing Scheme. [online] Available at: https://www.turing-scheme.org.uk/ [Accessed 29 Dec. 2022].

van Schaik, G., 2022. Can business schools rescue business?. In The Value & Purpose of Management Education (pp. 42–49). Routledge.

Winter, E., Costello, A., O'Brien, M. and Hickey, G., 2021. Teachers' use of technology and the impact of Covid-19. Irish Educational Studies, 40(2), pp.235-246.

Wong, L.W., Tan, G.W.H., Hew, J.J., Ooi, K.B. and Leong, L.Y., 2022. Mobile social media marketing: a new marketing channel among digital natives in higher education?. Journal of Marketing for Higher Education, 32(1), pp.113-137.

About the Author

Stephen James BA(Hons), QTS, FRSA

Stephen James is a highly qualified and experienced educator, earning a BA (Hons) in Primary Education from Canterbury Christ Church University and achieving QTS (Qualified Teacher Status). He has also been recognized as a Specialist Leader of Education and a Maths Specialist for the National Centre of Excellence in Teaching Mathematics. Throughout his career, Stephen has consistently demonstrated outstanding leadership and teaching practice, leading to recognition and awards such as Kent Teacher of the Year in 2018 and 2021.

In addition to his educational pursuits, Stephen has a unique background in military and intelligence operations, where he developed expertise in social networking and information operations. He has worked with various intelligence organizations, including GCHQ, 15 Psychological (UK) Operations Group, and the CIA.

Stephen is the founder and CEO of Social Media for Schools, a social media marketing agency for schools, and co-founder of Invicta National Academy, which provided millions of minutes of free catch-up learning to children during the Covid lockdowns. His efforts during the pandemic earned him recognition as an "Educational Hero" by the Chairman of the Education Select Committee and praise from the Secretary of State for Education in the House of Commons, leading to his invitation to become a Fellow of the Royal Society for Arts, Manufactures and Commerce.

In addition to his work with Social Media for Schools, Stephen is a Business Mentor for Finito Education, supporting young people in finding meaningful careers, and the founder of British Veteran Owned, a Community Interest Company providing a national accreditation scheme to support veterans through meaningful business interactions.

You can connect with me on:

- https://socialmediaforschools.co.uk
- https://twitter.com/SMforSchoolsUK
- https://www.facebook.com/SMforSchoolsUK
- https://www.instagram.com/smforschoolsuk
- https://www.linkedin.com/company/social-media-for-schools-uk

www.ingramcontent.com/pod-product-compliance
Lightning Source LLC
Chambersburg PA
CBHW051004060726
47593CB00017B/1058